BOOKWORMS

Transformations in Nature

A Larva
Becomes a Fly

Amy Hayes

T0014537

Cavendish
Square

New York

Published in 2016 by Cavendish Square Publishing, LLC
243 5th Avenue, Suite 136, New York, NY 10016

First Edition

Website: cavendishsq.com

This publication represents the opinions and views of the author based on his or her personal experience, knowledge, and research. The information in this book serves as a general guide only. The author and publisher have used their best efforts in preparing this book and disclaim liability rising directly or indirectly from the use and application of this book.

CPSIA Compliance Information: Batch #CW16CSQ

All websites were available and accurate when this book was sent to press.

Cataloging-in-Publication Data

Hayes, Amy.
A larvae becomes a fly / by Amy Hayes.
p. cm. — (Transformations in nature)
Includes index.
ISBN 978-1-5026-0832-1 (hardcover) ISBN 978-1-5026-0830-7 (paperback) ISBN 978-1-5026-0833-8 (e-book)
1. Flies — Juvenile literature. 2. Flies — Life cycles — Juvenile literature. I. Hayes, Amy. II. Title.
QL533.2 H39 2016
595.77'4—d23

Editorial Director: David McNamara
Copy Editor: Rebecca Rohan
Art Director: Jeffrey Talbot
Designer: Stephanie Flecha
Senior Production Manager: Jennifer Ryder-Talbot
Production Editor: Renni Johnson
Photo Research: J8 Media

Printed in the United States of America

Contents

A **larva** turns into a fly.

More than one larva are called **larvae**.

First, a mother lays her eggs.

The eggs hatch into larvae.

11

Larvae eat and eat
for about a week.

Larvae that are full make a red **covering**.

15

This red shell is
called a **pupa**.

After a few weeks,
the pupa breaks open.

19

A fly comes out!

21

New Words

covering (KOV-er-ing) Something that goes over the larva to protect it.

larva (LAR-va) A very young insect that looks like a worm.

larvae (LAR-vay) More than one larva.

pupa (PEW-pa) Insects in a transformation stage, usually inside a cocoon.

Index

About the Author

Amy Hayes lives in the beautiful city of Buffalo, New York. She has written several books for children, including *Hornets*, *Medusa and Pegasus*, *From Wax to Crayons*, and *We Need Worms!*

About BOOK WORMS

Bookworms help independent readers gain reading confidence through high-frequency words, simple sentences, and strong picture/text support. Each book explores a concept that helps children relate what they read to the world they live in.